INSPIRING ARTISTS
LEONARDO DA VINCI

Franklin Watts

First published in Great Britain in 2015 by
The Watts Publishing Group

Editor: Julia Bird
Design: Mark Ruffle/www.rufflebrothers.co.uk
Page layout: sprout.uk.com

ISBN 978 1 4451 4543 3

Dewey number: 750

Printed in China

Franklin Watts
An imprint of
Hachette Children's Group
Part of The Watts Publishing Group
Carmelite House
50 Victoria Embankment
London EC4Y 0DZ

An Hachette UK Company
www.hachette.co.uk

www.franklinwatts.co.uk

INSPIRING ARTISTS

LEONARDO DA VINCI

PAUL ROCKETT

W
FRANKLIN WATTS
LONDON•SYDNEY

Picture acknowledgements: Front cover, 3, 25t; Portrait of Cecilia Gallerani, Lady with the Ermine c.1488. Czartoryski Museum Cracow. Oil on wood, 54.8 x 40.3 cm. 6; Francesco Melzi, Portrait of Leonardo in profile, c.1515. Royal Collection Trust, © Her Majesty The Queen/Bridgeman Art Library. Red chalk on paper, 27.5 x 19cm. 7t; Lorenzo Rosselli atrrib. Carta della Catena, c.1471-1482. Museo de Firenze Com'era/ Iberfoto/Superstock. 7b; Verrochio, Bust of Lorenzo Medici, c.1480. National Gallery Of Art, Washington DC. Painted terracotta, 65.8 x 59.1 x 32.7cm. 8bl; Verrochio, Head of Woman, 1475. The British Museum, London. Charcoal and ink, 32.4 x 27.3cm. 8br; Study for Head of Leda c.1504-06. Royal Library, Windsor. Ink and chalk on paper, 17.7 x 14.7 cm. 9; Verrochio and Leonardo, The Baptism of Christ, c.1472-1475. Uffizi Gallery, Florence/Leemage/Corbis. Oil and tempera on wood, 177 x 151 cm. 10t; Star of Bethlehem and other plants. Codex Windsor. Pen and ink over red chalk on paper, 19.8 x 16cm. 10b; The Annuciation, 1472-1475. Galleria della Uffizi, Firenze. Oil and tempera on wood, 98 x 217 cm. 11t; Design for a flying machine c.1488, Codex Atlanticus, f 858 r. Biblioteca Ambrosiana, Milan. Ink on paper, 64.5 x 43.5cm. 11b; John William Waterhouse, The Annunciation, 1914. Private collection. Oil on canvas, 135 x 99 cm. 12; Landscape of the Arno Valley, 1473. Uffizi Gallery, Florence. Ink on paper, 19 x 28.5 cm. 13t, 13bl & 36br details; Ginevra de' Benci, 1474–1478. National Gallery of Art, Washington DC. Oil on wood, 38.1 x 37cm. 13br; JMW Turner, Norham Castle, Sunrise, c.1845. Tate Britain/Stefano Ravera/SuperStock. Oil on canvas, 90.8 x 121.9 cm. 14; Hugo van der Goes, Portinari Alterpiece, 1482 central panel. Galleria della Uffizi, Firenze. Oil on wood, 253 x 304cm. 15tl, 15tr detail; The Madonna of the Carnation, 1478–1480. Alte Pinothek, Munich/SuperStock. Oil on wood, 62 x 48 cm. 16l; Study of Madonna and Child with Cat, c.1478. The British Museum, London. Ink on paper, 281 x 199 cm. 16br; Madonna of the Yarnwinder, c.1499. Private collection. Oil on wood, 50.2 x 36.4 cm. 17t; Study of a Rearing Horse, c.1503. Royal Library, Windsor. Heritage /SuperStock. Red chalk and pencil,15.3 x 14.2 cm. 17b; Carla Carrà, The Red Horseman, 1913. © DACS 2015, Museo da Novecento, Milan/Bridgeman Art Library. Tempera and ink on paper, 26 x 36 cm. 18; Adoration of the Magi, 1481. Uffizi Gallery, Florence. Oil on wood, 246 x 243 cm. 19t; St John the Baptist, 1513–1516. The Louvre, Paris. Oil on wood, 69 x 57 cm. 19b; Rembrandt, Self-Portrait as a Young Man, c.1628. Rijksmuseum, Amsterdam. Oil on wood, 22.6 x 18.7cm. 20cl; Ambrogio de Predis, miniature of Ludovico Sforza from Codex Sforza, c.1495. Biblioteca Trivulzio, Milan. Pigment on paper. 20bl; Chariot and tank sketch, c.1487. The British Museum, London. Alinari Archive/Corbis. Ink on paper, 17.3 x 24.5 cm. 20r; Sketch of giant crossbow, c. 1485. Codex Atlanticus f 149a. Everett Historical/Shutterstock. Ink on paper, 64.5 x 43.5 cm. 21t; Bridge sketch, c.1502. Paris ms, f.65v and 66r. Bibliotheque Nationale, Paris. Ink on paper, 65 x 42 cm. 21b; The Da Vinci Bridge, Ås, Norway, Åsmund Ødegard, Norway. 22bl; St Jerome in the Wilderness, c.1480–1482. Vatican Museums. Tempera and oil on wood, 103 x 75 cm. 22tr; Anatomical Studies of a Male Shoulder, c.1509-1510. Royal Library Windsor, GraficaArtis/Corbis. Ink on paper, 29.2 x19.8 cm. 23t; Anatomical Studies of the Larynx and Leg, 1510. Royal Library Windsor, Janaka Dhamasena/ Dreamstime. Ink on paper, 28.9 x 19.8 cm. 23b; Vesalius, Anatomy Study from Vesalius's Fabrica, 1543. 24bl; Study of Five Grotesque Heads, c.1492. Royal Library Windsor. Ink on paper, 21.6 x 20.6 cm. 24tr; Quentin Matsys, The Ugly Duchess, 1513. The National Gallery, London/SuperStock. Oil on wood, 64.2 x 45.5 cm. 25b; Awol Erizku, Lady With Pitbull, 2009. © the Artist. Photograph. 26t; Euro coin with image of Vitruvian Man. Jakub Krechowicz/ Shutterstock. 26b; Vitruvian Man, c.1492. Galleria dell'Accademia, Venice. Ink on paper, 34 x 26 cm. 27l; On Divine Proportions by Luca Pacioli, illustration by Leonardo, c.1498. Private Collection/Bridgeman Art Library, lithograph. 27r; Piet Mondrian, Composition with Red, Yellow and Blue, 1930. Kunsthaus, Zurich. Oil on canvas, 46 x 46 cm. 28, 29t; The Last Supper, 1495–1498, Convent of Santa Maria delle Grazie, Milan. Oil, tempera, fresco, 460 x 880 cm. 29b; Rembrandt, The Wedding of Samson, 1638. Gemaldegallerie Dresden. Oil on canvas,126 x 176cm. 30; The Virgin and Child with St Anne and John the Baptist, 1508–1509. The National Gallery, London/SuperStock. Charcoal and chalk on paper, 142 x 105 cm. 31t; The Virgin and Child with St Anne and a Lamb, c.1508–1510, The Louvre, Paris. Oil on wood,168 x 112 cm. 31b; Max Ernst, The Kiss, 1927. © ADAGP, Paris and DACS, London 2015. Peggy Guggenheim Collection, Venice/Bridgeman Art Library. Oil on canvas, 129x 161 cm. 32bl; Michelangelo, David, 1501–1504. Veniamin Kraskov/Shutterstock. Marble h 434cm. 32tr; Study of battles on horseback and on foot, 1503–1504. Galleria Dell'Academia, Venice. Pen and ink on paper, 16 x 15.2 cm. 33t; Sangallo after Michelangelo, Scene from The Battle of Cascina, 1542. Holkham Hall, Norfolk. Oil on wood, 77 x 130cm. 33b; Rubens after Leonardo, Scene from The Battle of Anghiari, 1603. The Louvre, Paris. Chalk and ink on paper, 45.3 x 63.3 cm. 34; Andy Warhol, Thirty Are Better Than One, 1963. © 2015 The Andy Warhol Foundation for the Visual Arts, Inc./Artists Rights Society (ARS), New York and DACS, London. Peter Brandt Collection/Corbis Images. Silkscreen on canvas, 279.4 x 238.8 cm. 35,36bl detail; Mona Lisa, 1503–1517, The Louvre, Paris. Oil on wood,77 x 53 cm. 37; Gerhard Richter, Betty, 1977. © 2013 Gerhard Richter. All rights reserved. Oil on canvas, 50 x 40 cm. 38bl; Raphael, Lady with a Unicorn, c.1506. Galleria Borghese, Rome. Oil on wood, 65 x 61 cm. 38br; Raphael, Canigiani Holy Family, c.1507. Alte Pinakothek, Munich. Oil on wood, 131 x 107 cm, 39l; Salai, Head of Christ, c.1511. Pinacoteca Ambrosiana, Milan/Bridgeman Art Library. Oil on wood, 57 x 37.5 cm, 39tr; Francesco Melzi, Leda and the Swan, c.1508-15. Uffizi Gallery, Florence. Oil on wood, 130 x 77.5 cm. 40; Virgin of the Rocks, 1483–1486. The Louvre, Paris/Getty Images. Oil on wood, 199 x 122cm. 41; Virgin of the Rocks, 1506-1508. The National Gallery, London/De Agostini/ SuperStock. Oil on wood,189.5 x 120 cm. 42l; Portrait of a Bearded Man, 1512. Biblioteca Reale, Turin/SuperStock. Chalk on paper, 33.3 x 21.6 cm. 42tr; The Deluge, c.1517-1518. Codex Atlanticus, Biblioteca Ambrosiana, Milan. Ink on paper. 43t; Ingres, Death of Da Vinci, 1818. Musée de Petit Palais, Paris. Oil on canvas, 400 x 505 cm. 43b; Maggi Hambling, Wall of Water VII, 2011. Photo Douglas Atfield. © Maggi Hambling. Oil on canvas, 198.12 x 226.06cm.

CONTENTS

LEONARDO AND 15TH CENTURY FLORENCE

Leonardo da Vinci was born on 15 April, 1452. He is now known as an inventor, engineer, scientist, musician and architect, but he is most famous for being an artist. His remarkable talents made him a celebrity during his lifetime and an inspiration to many artists both then and since.

YOUNG DA VINCI

Leonardo da Vinci's surname 'da Vinci' means 'of Vinci', the name of the small Italian town in Tuscany where he was born, the illegitimate son of a local lawyer and a young peasant woman. Little is known about Leonardo's early life. He moved to the nearby city of Florence when he was around the age of 17 to work.

FLOURISHING FLORENCE

Florence was an exciting city to be an artist or craftsman in the 15th century. An independent city, it was experiencing a period of great wealth thanks to the booming textile and banking trades. This wealth was invested back into the city by Florence's citizens and the Church, who supported the work of its artists by constructing spectacular buildings and commissioning many works of art to decorate them.

A Portrait of Leonardo in Profile, c.1515, Francesco Melzi

A view of the city of Florence in the 15th century.

THE RENAISSANCE

Florence was considered to be at the heart of a movement called the Renaissance. Renaissance means 'rebirth' and describes a period from around the mid-14th to the late 16th century, when people looked to the past cultures of Ancient Greece (5th to 2nd centuries BCE) and Rome (5th century BCE to 5th century CE) for learning and inspiration. The Renaissance focused on human experience, realism and emotion in art. It was also a time of great exploration, with new continents being discovered, while huge advances were made in the studies of science and astronomy.

Portrait bust of Lorenzo de' Medici, Verrocchio, 1480

THE HOUSE OF MEDICI

The wealthy Medici dynasty was one of the most powerful families in Florence in the 15th century. Lorenzo de' Medici (1449–1492) was a great lover of the arts and supported them through a system known as patronage. This involved sponsoring artists and scientists in return for the status gained from supporting the top talent of the day. Leonardo spent much of his life supported by wealthy patrons such as Lorenzo de' Medici.

THE ARTIST'S WORKSHOP

In 1469 Leonardo was sent to train as an apprentice at the busy workshop of the artist and sculptor Andrea del Verrocchio (1435–1488). Workshops in Florence were filled with young aspiring artists. They worked hard for a living, learning how to grind pigment for paints and make paintbrushes, among many other tasks. They served a long apprenticeship before becoming an assistant.

VERROCCHIO

Andrea del Verrocchio worked for a time under the patronage of the Medici family. He produced paintings and designed armour, but was most celebrated for his bronze sculptures. His students would have been greatly influenced by his work, as they would have studied it in close detail. Some of the poses Leonardo later used in his paintings can be found in the work of Verrocchio.

COLLABORATIONS

Artists' workshops were collaborative and assistants often helped to finish some of their master's work. After his apprenticeship, Leonardo stayed on as an assistant in Verrocchio's workshop, where his earliest known painting was completed together with his master.

In the painting *The Baptism of Christ* (opposite) Leonardo is believed to have completed the angel on the left. The painting work here appears softer, with a more subtle use of colour compared to the other figures. So impressed was Verrocchio by Leonardo's contribution that it's said he vowed never to paint again – stunned at how an assistant could be so much better than his master.

ART SPOT *One of these drawings below is by Verrocchio and the other by Leonardo. What similarities in the pose and detail can you see?*

Head of a Woman, Verrocchio, 1475

The Head of Leda, Leonardo, c.1504–1506

The Baptism of Christ, Verrocchio and Leonardo, c.1472–1475

NATURE LOVER

The work that Leonardo completed while at Verrocchio's workshop is outstanding in its realistic representation of nature. Throughout his life, Leonardo filled sketchbooks with studies of wildlife (right) and water, recording tiny details. Nature was his biggest inspiration, and he spent much of his life trying to capture its workings.

'Nature is the source of all true knowledge. She has her own logic, her own laws, she has had no effect without cause nor invention without necessity.' –Leonardo

Star of Bethlehem and Other Plants, c.1505–1510

PLANT LIFE

The painting *The Annunciation* (below) was completed while Leonardo was at Verrocchio's workshop. The painting shows a story from the Bible, where the Angel Gabriel appears before the Virgin Mary to tell her that she will become the mother of Jesus, the Son of God. Leonardo's knowledge of nature can be seen here in the depiction of the plants, which contains as much detail as the main figures.

WATER

Leonardo observed nature in the same way as today's scientists and engineers. He made lots of drawings and notes on water. He wanted to know what determined its flow and how to control it. He later designed locks and canal systems, and investigated the possibility of redirecting a section of the River Arno away from Pisa.

The Annunciation, 1472–1475

WINGS

The wings attached to the angel in *The Annunciation* have been carefully studied from birds, and suggest the beginnings of Leonardo's obsession with flight. His books are filled with sketches of wings and designs of flying machines. It is believed that he bought caged birds and set them free to study their flight.

THE PRE-RAPHAELITE BROTHERHOOD

The Pre-Raphaelites, a group of artists that formed in 1848 in England, shared Leonardo's desire to capture nature realistically. They looked to pre-16th century art, including the work of the Renaissance, for inspiration. Members, who included John William Waterhouse (1849–1917) and John Everett Millais (1829–1896) visited Italy and studied Leonardo's paintings, including his *Annunciation*. Waterhouse went on to paint his own version of the scene.

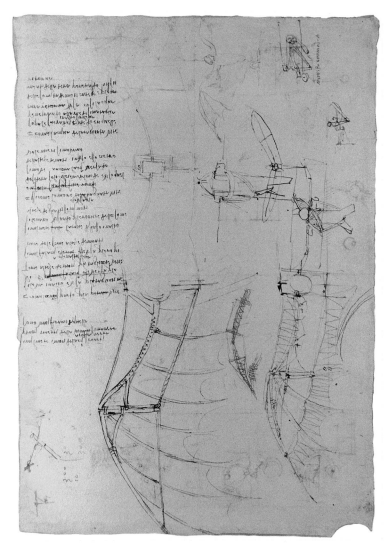

The Annunciation, John William Waterhouse, 1914

Design for a Flying Machine, c.1488

LANDSCAPES

Leonardo's fascination with nature went beyond the observation of individual plants to studying landscapes. He wanted to see how natural processes, such as the water cycle, impacted on the wider environment and looked for ways to represent these in his painting.

TUSCANY

Leonardo grew up in Tuscany, a region with spectacular landscapes of rolling hills, deep valleys, and the dramatic Apennine Mountains towering in the north. This scenery was to have a strong impact on the landscapes that appear in his paintings.

FIRST LANDSCAPE DRAWING

Tuscany is captured in Leonardo's earliest known drawing, *Landscape of the Arno Valley*, dated 5 August, 1473. The sketch is often labelled as 'the first landscape drawing in Western art', as up until this time artwork had mainly been of religious subjects and portraits. It appears as though drawn quickly on location, with the artist following the journey of a waterfall down towards floodplains and the farmland in the distance.

Landscape of the Arno Valley, 1473

AERIAL PERSPECTIVE

Leonardo's studies of landscapes led him to observe that when an object, such as a mountain, was further away, its outline became fuzzier and its colour cooler and bluer. He concluded that this was because the quantity of atmosphere (moisture and dust) increased between the mountain and the viewer. He named this effect 'aerial perspective' – a term and technique still applied today. The use of aerial perspective can be spotted in one of Leonardo's earliest paintings, *Ginevra de' Benci* (left).

TURNER

The effects of aerial perspective can be seen pushed to their limits within the paintings of Joseph Mallord William Turner (1775–1851). Turner used the technique to paint landscapes that appear as fuzzy patches of colour and light, rather than as solid physical forms, as can be seen in *Norham Castle, Sunrise* (below).

Ginevra de' Benci, c.1474–1478

The use of aerial perspective here makes the trees and hills in the background look far away.

Norham Castle, Sunrise, JMW Turner, c.1845

THE NETHERLANDISH INFLUENCE

Leonardo was experimenting with new techniques and materials at the same time as artists in northern Europe. In 1483, a painting known as the *Portinari Altarpiece* by Netherlandish artist Hugo van der Goes (1440 –1482), arrived in Florence. The painting had a huge effect on the city's painters, who praised its realism and sought to copy its style.

OIL PAINTS

The *Portinari Altarpiece* shows the shepherds (top right) visiting the baby Jesus at the stable in Bethlehem. It made use of the newly popular oil paints. Before, painters largely used an opaque medium known as tempera that dried quickly and dulled the colours. Oil paints allowed for more subtle, translucent layers, richer, more brilliant colours and a glossy surface. They also took a long time to dry so artists could spend longer adding finer details.

ATTENTION TO DETAIL

During the Renaissance, artists from the Netherlands tried to make objects appear as real as possible. In the *Portinari Altarpiece* great attention is given to textures and small objects, such as hair, a shoe, a piece of straw. The faithful depictions of the flowers in the foreground are similar to Leonardo's efforts in *The Annunciation* (see p.10) and the *Madonna of the Carnation* (opposite).

Portinari Altarpiece, Hugo van der Goes, 1475

Madonna of the Carnation, 1478–1480

The vase has been painted over the background with thin layers of oil paint. Heavier layers of white outline the pattern on the vase, while also acting as reflections of light. These add to its glassy appearance.

TEXTURE AND LIGHT

Van der Goes used a technique of building up translucent layers that helped him to create more realistic textures and light effects. Leonardo began to do this in the *Madonna of the Carnation*. There is a softer texture to the cushion compared to the clothes, and small details of light are used to give shape to objects, such as the rays bouncing off the brooch and the pattern on the vase.

SYMBOLISM

The objects in van der Goes' and Leonardo's paintings were carefully chosen as symbols connected to the paintings' subject. Each of the flowers has a religious meaning: the violets symbolise modesty; lilies and irises represent the passion and sorrow of the Madonna; red carnations represent the blood of Christ and the translucent vase shows the purity of the Madonna (see p.45 for more explanation of this and selected other works).

DYNAMIC SKETCHING

By 1478 Leonardo had left Verrocchio's workshop and set up on his own. He now had more freedom to follow his interests and develop his own techniques. Leonardo began sketching people at work and animals at play. By doing so, he was investigating their natural movements.

NATURAL POSES

In Leonardo's sketches and paintings of the Madonna and Child, the child (Jesus) is often distracted and wriggly. This is realistic of how a child behaves, and a movement away from the stiffness seen in early paintings. By showing the world as a moving, living thing, Leonardo is able to make his figures appear much more lifelike. He also makes the holy figures of Madonna and Jesus much more human.

Madonna of the Yarnwinder, c.1499

Study of Madonna and Child with a Cat, c.1478

CAPTURING MOVEMENT

In *Study of Madonna and Child with a Cat* it looks like the figures of the child and cat are struggling to stay still. Lots of lines are marked over each other, suggesting their movements. These lines helped Leonardo decide which position the figures should take in the final piece of work.

FUTURISM

Leonardo's investigations of movement influenced Futurism, an art movement from the early 20th century. Futurism celebrated ideas of the future, machines, objects of speed, force and dynamism. Although Futurists rejected art from the past, they looked on Leonardo as a honorary Futurist. They saw much of his work as being about progress and moving forwards. They admired his proposed machines (see p.20–21), as well as his studies on movement.

ART SPOT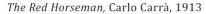
Compare the drawing of a horse by Leonardo (right) to the painting below by Futurist artist Carlo Carrà (1881–1966). What similarities are there? What do you think both artists were trying to capture?

Study of a Rearing Horse, c.1503

The Red Horseman, Carlo Carrà, 1913

LIGHT AND DARK

Around 1481, Leonardo was commissioned to paint the *Adoration of the Magi* for the altar of a monastery near Florence. It depicts the three magi (kings) kneeling down in worship before Mary and Jesus. The painting was not finished but it stands as one of his masterpieces, a complex work that displays his skill in modelling figures with light and dark effects, known as *chiaroscuro*.

Adoration of the Magi, 1481

ART SPOT

Why do you think Leonardo made the figures in the background of Adoration of the Magi *much darker than those in the foreground?*

CHIAROSCURO

Chiaroscuro is Italian for 'light' (*chiaro*) and 'dark' (*scuro*). It is a technique that Leonardo developed himself, which uses an extreme contrast of light and dark tones. In the *Adoration of the Magi* the darkest areas push the space back, creating a sense of depth. The light areas pick out features on the figures that make them stand out and appear almost three-dimensional.

IN THE SPOTLIGHT

Leonardo's use of chiaroscuro can be seen most dramatically in his later painting *St John the Baptist*. Here, the figure is emerging from the darkness into the light, with Leonardo using just enough light for us to make out the whole of his body. Leonardo's use of chiaroscuro had a great influence on painting. Its impact can clearly be seen in the works of later artists such as Caravaggio (1571–1610) and Rembrandt (1606–1669).

St John the Baptist, c.1513–1516

REMBRANDT

The 17th century Dutch painter Rembrandt sometimes shaped his portraits with dark shadows falling across their faces. This can have the effect of distancing the subject from the viewer, and gives an impression of a subject lost in their thoughts.

Self Portrait as a Young Man, Rembrandt, c.1628

MILAN AND ENGINEERING EFFORTS

In 1482, Leonardo left Florence for the court of the future Duke of Milan, Ludovico Sforza. Here, he was to work not only as a painter but also as an engineer and designer of all kinds of machines, including ones for waging war.

DESIGNING MACHINES

In Milan Leonardo explored many ideas for hydraulic systems, canals, submarines and flying machines. He was also busy with designs of military machines, such as mortars, mines, chariots, giant crossbows and an early type of tank. Although none were built during his lifetime, his skills as an artist meant that his designs dazzled those that saw them, while the promise of great future machinery helped to keep him in employment.

Crossbow sketch, c.1485

DIVIDED

During the Renaissance, Italy was not a unified country. It was made up of independent city-states with their own rulers and armies. There was much fighting between the cities, and, towards the end of the 15th century, there was also a threat of invasion from France. A show of strength through weapons was important for the defence of each city-state. This is what Leonardo aimed to bring to Milan.

Detail of Ludovico Sforza from the Sforza Altarpiece, Bembo, c.1495

Chariot and tank sketch, c.1487

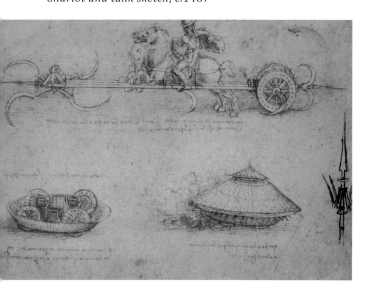

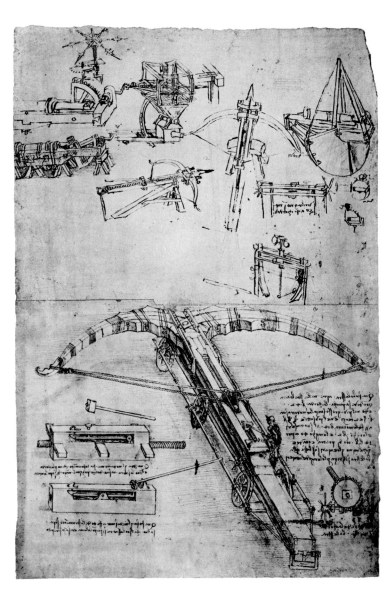

THE DA VINCI BRIDGE

In 1996, Norwegian artist Vebjørn Sand (1966–) came across a sketch for a bridge in one of Leonardo's notebooks. Impressed by its design, he set about making it a reality. Leonardo's bridge was designed to cross the Golden Horn inlet at Istanbul, Turkey. It would have been the world's longest bridge at that time, measuring 346 metres in length. Sand scaled down the bridge to around a third of the original size, and built it as a footbridge. The bridge was finally unveiled in 2001 near the town of Ås in Norway, 500 years after Leonardo had made his design.

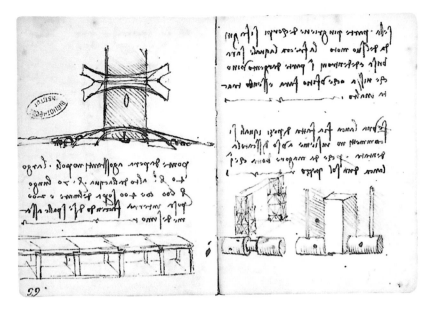

Golden Horn Bridge sketch, c.1502

The Da Vinci Bridge, Ås, Norway

ANATOMICAL STUDIES

Leonardo produced his first studies of the human body while in Milan. It was an important time for medical science, with new discoveries in human biology being made. Leonardo's desire to understand the workings of the body helped his art, and put him at the forefront of scientific discovery.

SKIN AND BONES

Leonardo often drew his figures naked so that he could get the shape of the bodies right before he clothed them. In his unfinished painting, *St Jerome in the Wilderness*, it looks as though Leonardo has drawn the saint's muscles

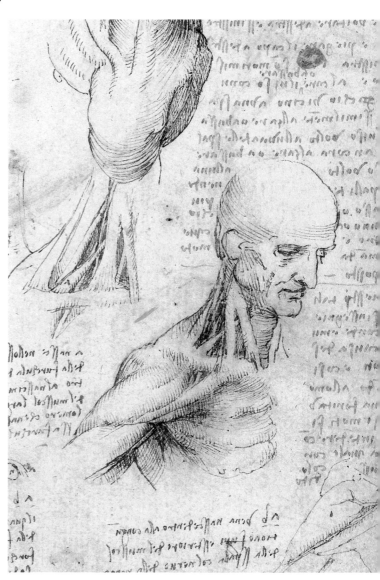

Studies of the Shoulder and Neck, c.1509–1510

and bones first. St Jerome is an historical figure who went to lead a simple life in the desert, taking few clothes and possessions with him. The cloak draped over his shoulder in the painting appears almost like another layer of skin.

 **ART SPOT** *What impact does seeing the bones, muscles and tendons of St Jerome have on our understanding of his story?*

St Jerome in the Wilderness, c.1480

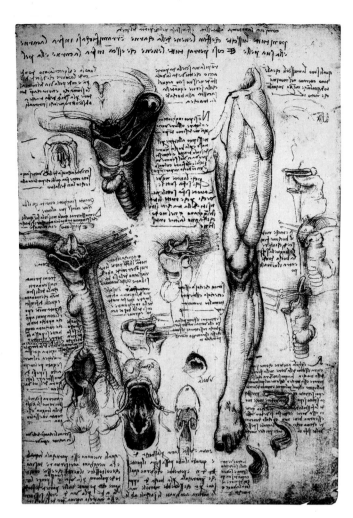

INSIDE THE BODY

Leonardo's desire to learn more about the workings of the human body led him to study the body's internal organs, such as the brain, heart and lungs. To do this, he visited hospitals and mortuaries to dissect corpses. Cutting into the body allowed Leonardo to make groundbreaking observations. He discovered how the heart functions and learned how blood flows through its valves. He dissected around 30 corpses, making a collection of anatomical drawings that showed an understanding of the human body that had not existed before.

Studies of the larynx (throat) and leg, c.1510

FATHER OF MODERN ANATOMY

In 1543, the anatomist Andreas Vesalius (1514–1564) published a book called *The Fabric of the Human Body*, which was filled with illustrations and observations on human biology. Like Leonardo, he had learned much from dissecting human corpses. The influence of Vesalius' book led him to be known as the 'father of modern anatomy'. However, many argue that this title should go to Leonardo. Although Leonardo's studies were not published during his lifetime, many believe that Vesalius had seen them as they contain many similarities.

Muscle Man, Vesalius, 1543

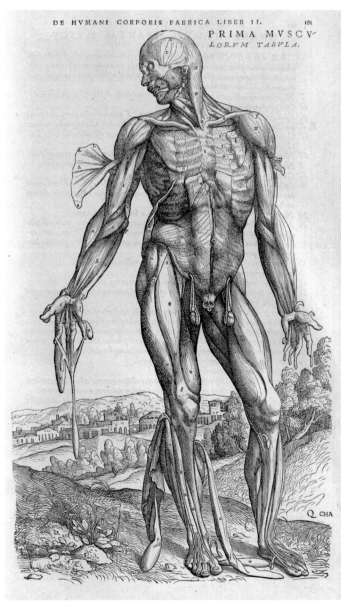

THE BEAUTIFUL AND THE GROTESQUE

Leonardo believed that all things in nature should be observed. Just as he felt it was important to study both the outside and the inside of the human body, he also wanted to record both beautiful and ugly people.

DELIGHT IN DIFFERENCE

Leonardo took delight in drawing people with features that looked unusual and grotesque. He used to follow people with strange faces around the streets of Milan, making sketches of them. His fascination with ugliness was unusual at a time when most artists were looking to represent an ideal of beauty, and could be seen as an attempt to highlight the opposite of beauty.

The Ugly Duchess, Quentin Matsys, c.1513

Five Grotesque Heads, c.1500

ODD PASSION

Leonardo's interest in odd-looking faces is shared with the Netherlandish artist Quentin Matsys (1465/6–1530). It is thought that they wrote to each other, sending sketches and encouraging each other in their studies of what was perceived as grotesque. One of Matsys' most famous works was a portrait entitled *The Ugly Duchess* (above). It is believed that the sitter may have had a condition called Paget's disease, which enlarges and deforms the bones.

Lady with an Ermine, 1489–1490

ART SPOT *In 2009, Awol Erizku (1988–) updated the image of* Lady with an Ermine *with a photo of a young girl and a pitbull puppy. In what ways do you think her photo challenges ideas of beauty from the time of Leonardo?*

Lady with a Pitbull, Awol Erizku, 2009

PERFECT IMPERFECTIONS

Around 1489, Leonardo began work on *Lady with an Ermine*, a portrait believed to be of Ludovico Sforza's mistress, Cecilia Gallerani. There are different theories as to why she is holding an ermine (white stoat). Some experts think it was an emblem of Ludovico, others think that it was included as a pun on the model's surname – the ancient Greek name for ermine is *galê*. The portrait celebrates Cecilia's beauty. However, the right hand appears stretched in size. Others have spotted the detail of wrinkles on the hand, suggesting Leonardo did not seek to present her as all-round perfect.

DIVINE PROPORTIONS

Many people during the Renaissance, including Leonardo, looked for patterns in nature that could be represented as mathematical and geometrical formulas. These formulas were often included in their designs for buildings and compositions in art.

The image of the *Vitruvian Man* has become a symbol of the Renaissance and the ideal design of man. It appears on an Italian one Euro coin.

THE PROPORTIONS OF MAN

Leonardo's drawing *Vitruvian Man* has become an icon of the perfect man. It is named after an ancient Roman writer and architect,

Vitruvius (c.75 BCE–c.15 BCE), who looked to connect the laws of geometry with the ideal proportions of man. Leonardo's sketch illustrates Vitruvius' ideas, fitting man into both a square and a circle.

Vitruvian Man, c.1492

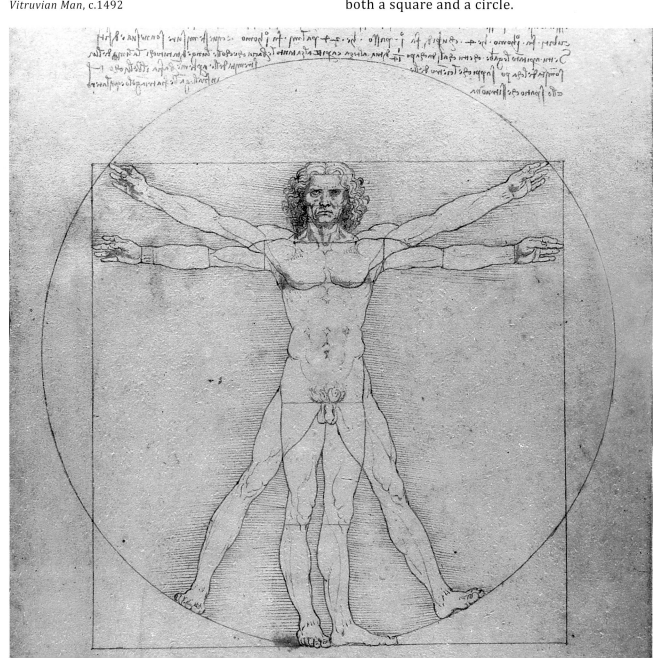

MATHS TUTORING

While in Milan, Leonardo was tutored in maths and geometry by Luca Pacioli (1445–1517). Pacioli was an expert mathematician, and became a long-term friend and collaborator of Leonardo. In around 1498, Pacioli was working on a book called *On Divine Proportion*. Leonardo worked alongside him, providing the illustrations and diagrams that would explain geometric concepts in architecture and the human body.

THE GOLDEN RULE

On Divine Proportion explored a theory known as the 'golden ratio'. This is a number that is used to calculate proportions in the creation of shapes. It is found by dividing a line into two parts, so that the longer part divided by the smaller part is also equal to the whole length divided by the longer part. It is often found in nature, for example in the way tree branches form. The belief is that by using the golden ratio in art and architecture, you create the most beautiful shapes and divisions of space. The golden ratio can be found in many paintings from the Renaissance and after, such as in the abstract works of the Dutch artist Piet Mondrian (1872–1944).

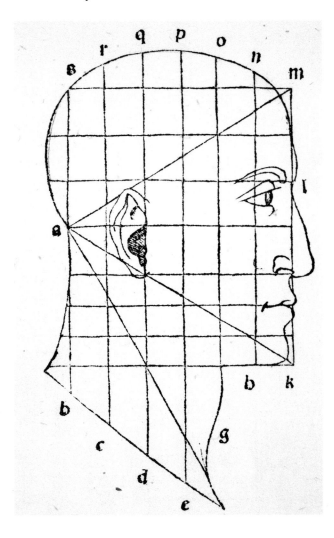

Proportions of a Human Head, from
On Divine Proportion, c.1498

Composition with Red, Blue and Yellow,
Piet Mondrian, 1930

ART SPOT *Many artists use the golden ratio and geometry in their work believing it to create a sense and balance and beauty. Do you think the Mondrian achieves this with his use of shapes in* Composition in Red, Blue and Yellow *(above right)?*

THE *LAST SUPPER*

In 1495, Leonardo began work on what many consider to be his greatest achievement, the *Last Supper*. This large wall painting captures the moment when Jesus has just announced that one of his disciples will betray him. The disciples around the table are shown responding in different dramatic poses, showing Leonardo's skill in representing movement and character.

PERSPECTIVE

The *Last Supper* is painted on a wall in the Santa Maria Delle Grazie convent in Milan. It is painted to look like an extension of the dining hall, with an illusion of depth created with the use of perspective grids. The lines that begin around the outside edge of the perspective grid all converge at a spot known as the 'vanishing point' (see opposite). These lines look as if they are disappearing into the distance, much in the same way the tracks of a railway line do, which seem to meet or vanish in the line of vision. Our eyes follow these lines towards the vanishing point, and in the *Last Supper* this point is on the head of Jesus. Placing the vanishing point here helps to make Jesus the focal point of the picture.

SHAPES AND NUMBERS

Leonardo has hidden shapes and numbers in the painting that add to its religious meaning. The figure of Jesus forms a triangular shape: a triangle and the number three are a symbol of the Holy Trinity (Father, Son and Holy Spirit). There are three windows behind Jesus and the disciples are also arranged into groups of three.

Last Supper, 1495–1498

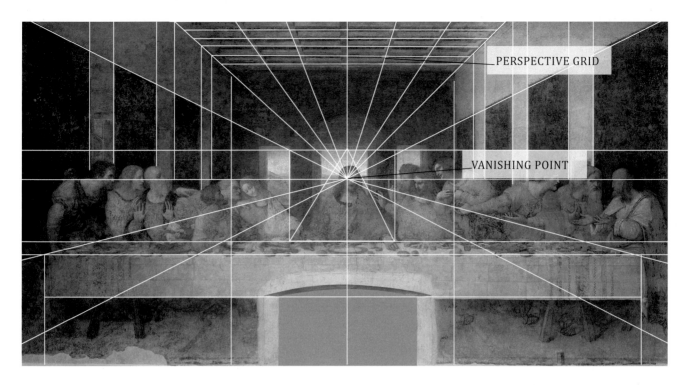

PERSPECTIVE GRID

VANISHING POINT

PEELING PAINT

Leonardo experimented with the mixture of his paint for the *Last Supper*, but it proved unsuitable for the damp convent wall and the paint started falling away within his lifetime. However, early viewers were astonished by the detail expressed in the faces and movement of each figure. The work has since been restored many times, but we are only left with an idea of its original power.

CARRYING ON THE COMPOSITION

The subject of the *Last Supper* is a challenge in how to arrange 13 men around a dinner table. Despite never seeing the original painting, Rembrandt was fascinated by this problem and made many sketches based on images of Leonardo's *Last Supper*, changing the grouping of the figures. Variations of this composition appear in Rembrandt's work, such as his painting *The Wedding of Samson*.

ART SPOT *Both Leonardo and Rembrandt looked to express the state of a person's mind through their movement. What do you think the figures in both paintings are feeling?*

The Wedding of Samson,
Rembrandt, 1638

RETURN TO FLORENCE

In 1499, the French army invaded Milan, causing Leonardo's patron, Ludovico, to flee the city. Leonardo left too, spending a short time in Venice before returning home to Florence. By this time, Leonardo's fame as a master artist and engineer had spread throughout Europe and he was greeted with much excitement.

BLOCKBUSTER EXHIBITION

In 1500, a large drawing by Leonardo went on public display in Florence. The drawing is now lost, but is thought to have been similar in subject and composition to his drawing *The Virgin and Child with St Anne and St John the Baptist.* This image shows Mary with her mother Anne, and Jesus, who is meeting John for the first time in the desert. The exhibited drawing attracted huge crowds. The 16th century art historian, Giorgio Vasari, described how the drawing:

'filled all artists with wonder [...] men and women, young and old, continued for two days to crowd into the room where it was exhibited, as if attending a solemn festival: and all were astonished at its excellence.'

The Virgin and Child with St Anne and St John the Baptist, c.1499–1500

PYRAMIDAL POSE

Leonardo's drawing and later painting *The Virgin and Child with St Anne* (right) both contain triangular shapes that group together the figures as a single unit. As with the *Last Supper*, this shape is used to represent the Holy Trinity, but here the triangles are more three-dimensional, creating what is called a 'pyramidal pose'. This pose became a standard structure in Renaissance paintings. As well as representing the Holy Trinity, it emphasises the strength and solidity of both the subject's character and its form.

SURREAL INTERPRETATION

These paintings of the Virgin Mary and Jesus, with their pyramidal pose, were the inspiration for a painting called *The Kiss*, by the Surrealist painter Max Ernst (1891–1976). *The Kiss,* like Leonardo's pictures, shows interconnected figures, but here they are loosely formed through a doodled wiggly line. This painting blurs the relationships between the figures – they appear almost as if they are one person. The title suggests that it represents the action of a kiss, but we cannot see one

The Virgin and Child with St Anne, c.1508–1510

taking place. Ernst had replaced the subject of religion with one of confused identity and family relationships.

The Kiss, Max Ernst, 1927

RENAISSANCE RIVALS

The art of the Renaissance is celebrated in the later work of Leonardo as well as the paintings and sculpture of a younger artist, Michelangelo (1475–1564). Each was considered to be a genius, however they were reputed to be less than dazzled by each other's reputations.

MIGHTY MICHELANGELO

Like Leonardo, Michelangelo was born in a small town near Florence and trained in the workshop of a Florentine artist. In 1504 he completed one of his most celebrated marble sculptures, *David* (right).

ARTISTIC DIFFERENCES

Michelangelo was more interested in and successful at sculpture than Leonardo, and both had different ideas of beauty in nature and art. Michelangelo was interested in representing the ideal physical form, making the bodies of his men big and broad with bulging muscles. Leonardo remarked in his notebook that:

'You should not make all the muscles of your figures obvious; even if they are shown in the correct place […] If you do otherwise you will have produced a sack of nuts rather than a human being.'

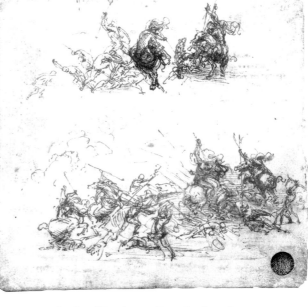

Study of Battles on Horseback and on Foot c.1504, a composition study for Leonardo's mural

AT BATTLE

In 1504, both Michelangelo and Leonardo were commissioned to paint murals of famous Florentine military victories that would face each other in Florence's main council hall. Whether it was planned as a contest is unclear, but bringing the work of Italy's two greatest living artists together is likely to have created a great deal of excitement and interest. However, both artists left the work unfinished. Leonardo left Florence to return to Milan and Michelangelo was summoned to Rome by the Pope to paint the ceiling of the Sistine Chapel.

David, Michelangelo, 1501–1504

A scene copied from Michelangelo's unfinished mural, *The Battle of Cascina*, da Sangallo, 1542

NEW WORKS

The work both artists had completed for the murals was later painted over by the painter, writer and architect Giorgio Vasari and his followers. They covered the original murals with battle scenes celebrating the new ruler, Cosimo I de Medici, after the fall of the Florentine republic in 1537. A recent discovery claims to have found a space behind one of Vasari's murals. It is hoped that Leonardo's original painting is hidden away in this space, and that it may soon be made visible once more.

A scene copied from Leonardo's unfinished mural, *The Battle of Anghiari*, Rubens, 1603

RUBENS

The Dutch painter Peter Paul Rubens (1577–1640) made a copy of Leonardo's *Battle of Anghiari*. He was inspired by its tight composition, and how it had captured the movement and action of the battle. Rubens painted many hunting and battle scenes built around the action of rearing horses, influenced by Leonardo's painting.

THE *MONA LISA*

While working on *The Battle of Anghiari*, Leonardo was also painting what is probably the most famous portrait painting in the world – the *Mona Lisa*. The expression of the figure, the curious background and the softly painted surface have mesmerised people for centuries.

THE *MONA LISA* SMILE

A great mystery surrounds the identity of the sitter – no one is entirely sure who the woman is. Another of the fascinations surrounding the *Mona Lisa* is the expression on her face. She is not fully smiling, and yet she has a look of amusement. It is as if Leonardo has caught her expression in mid-movement, just after turning round and laughing. This sense of something having occurred makes the painting appear to be more than just a snapshot in time.

SKILL AND TECHNIQUE

The *Mona Lisa* creates illusions of space and movement that draw the viewer in. The figure of the *Mona Lisa* appears as if she is sat next to the viewer, creating a sense of intimacy. This is achieved by putting her right at the front edge of the painting. She is framed by two columns, the bases of which we can just see. This tells us she is sat on a balcony. The background contains a dreamlike landscape. There is a higher horizon line to the right. To the left, the landscape is lower with water that slopes downwards. Along with the winding movement of the path, these differences of height suggest motion and a changing landscape.

ART SPOT *The curves in the river and the shape of the valley echo the curls of the sitter's hair and creases of her clothing. What do you think Leonardo was looking to achieve in doing this?*

LEGACY

The image of the *Mona Lisa* has been reproduced on postcards and in advertising all over the world. Its composition and technique have inspired many artists, such as Raphael (1483–1520) (see p.38) and Rembrandt (see p.19). However, some artists have used the image to poke fun at its iconic status. Pop artist Andy Warhol (1928–1987) created multiple prints of the *Mona Lisa* for his piece *Thirty Are Better than One*. Here Warhol questions the painting's overuse as an icon, reducing its original effect and impact.

Thirty Are Better than One, Andy Warhol, 1963

Mona Lisa, 1503–1517

VANISHING INTO SMOKE

Leonardo kept the *Mona Lisa* with him until his death, continually adding to it, making it one of his most detailed paintings. The length of time spent working on the painting allowed for him to perfect a technique he had been developing called *sfumato*.

SFUMATO

The *Mona Lisa* contains no hard lines or edges. Instead colours gently blend into each other, creating a subtle change in shape and form. This is the sfumato technique, which means 'vanishing in smoke', or in Leonardo's words, *'without lines or borders, in the manner of smoke'.* The subtle and gradual changes in tone have been carefully applied so that the painting's surface appears smooth, with no trace of brush marks.

The lack of lines outlining the features makes the Mona Lisa *appear more lifelike.*

UP CLOSE

Scientists have made investigations into how Leonardo achieved the sfumato effect. By taking X-rays of the *Mona Lisa*, they discovered 40 ultra-thin layers of paint. This tells us that it was achieved through a lengthy process, in which Leonardo carefully built up layers of fine detail. This may also explain why he spent so long on the painting.

ART SPOT *Leonardo started developing the sfumato technique early in his career. Compare the* Mona Lisa *with the portrait of Ginerva de' Benci below. How has his use of sfumato changed?*

In the portrait of Ginerva de' Benci, Leonardo had already started using the sfumato effect, but there are clearer lines around the eyelids and lighter skin tones.

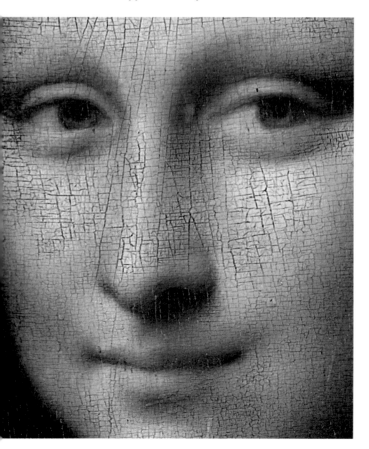

OUT OF FOCUS

German painter Gerhard Richter (1932–) creates a sfumato effect of extreme blurriness in some of his paintings. His painting *Betty* appears out-of-focus and has a smoothness similar to a photograph. Whereas Leonardo used sfumato to add to the feeling of being in front of a real person, Richter has applied it to the whole painting, creating a distance, like a veil, between the viewer and the figure painted.

Betty, Gerhard Richter, 1977

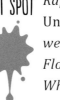

MASTER AND FOLLOWERS

Though Leonardo's output of artwork was small, slow and some was left unfinished, what he did produce attracted a great deal of attention and praise. People travelled a long way to see his work. Many young artists wanted to study under him and many others came to watch him at work in his studio.

RAPHAEL

In 1504, drawn by the stories of Leonardo's genius, the young up-and-coming painter Raphael Sanzio travelled from the town of Perugia to Florence. Here he met Leonardo and studied his paintings and drawings. Raphael's paintings are much brighter and more colourful than Leonardo's, but Leonardo's influence can clearly be seen in his poses and in the soft shading of sfumato.

'[Raphael] stood confounded in astonishment and admiration: the manner of da Vinci pleased him more than any other he had ever seen.'
– Giorgio Vasari

ART SPOT *Raphael's paintings the* Lady with a Unicorn *and the* Canigiani Holy Family *were both completed while he was in Florence at the same time as Leonardo. Which of Leonardo's paintings do you think their poses most resemble?*

Lady with a Unicorn, Raphael, c.1506

Canigiani Holy Family, Raphael, c.1507

PUPILS

Leonardo took in many apprentices and two became long-term companions. Salaì (1480–1524) joined Leonardo's household in 1490. Leonardo made many sketches of Salai and it is thought that he was the model for *St John the Baptist* (see p.19). Francesco Melzi (1491–1570) became his apprentice in 1506. Both produced work in similar styles to Leonardo, as well as copying his paintings. Neither was as talented as Leonardo, though they may have had a hand in his later work. Salaì's *Head of Christ* (below) is believed to be a self-portrait. The face shows the light, shade and soft colours that Leonardo used to make his figures lifelike.

Head of Christ, Salaì, c.1511

Leda and the Swan, Francesco Melzi, c.1508–1515

LEDA AND THE SWAN

In around 1506, Leonardo completed a painting called *Leda and the Swan*. The painting shows a scene from an ancient Greek myth, where the god Zeus seduces Leda in the form of a swan. Her children are seen hatching beside her. The painting is now lost, possibly destroyed. However the original inspired many copies, including a sketch made by Raphael. Melzi, a more talented painter than Salaì, made a copy of the painting, which for a time some mistook for the original painting by Leonardo.

THE TWO *VIRGIN OF THE ROCKS*

In 1506 Leonardo began work on a painting called *Virgin of the Rocks* – a copy of a painting he had made 20 years before. The owners of the original painting had fallen out with Leonardo over payment and it is likely the second painting was produced to settle this dispute. The two paintings have caused debates over which best shows Leonardo's talent, which came first and whether he even raised his brush to one of them.

ART SPOT *What differences can you see between the two paintings? Which do you think is the better of the two and why?*

Virgin of the Rocks, 1483–1486

SUBJECT

The paintings show an imagined meeting between Jesus and St John the Baptist. Both have left Bethlehem to escape King Herod's massacre of young children (Gospel of Matthew, chapter 2, verses 13–23), and with Mary and the Angel Uriel, sit together, forming a pyramidal pose (see p.31). The Angel Uriel has brought John, who sits in prayer next to Mary. Jesus is sat next to Uriel with his hand raised in blessing towards John.

SPOT THE DIFFERENCE

The distance in time between the two paintings suggests that we should be able to see a development in Leonardo's style. Both paintings show his techniques of sfumato and aerial perspective, but the use of chiaroscuro appears more extreme in the painting on the right. This painting is generally accepted as being the later version, though its differences have led some experts to doubt Leonardo's involvement in this painting. Most agree, however, that the Angel Uriel was painted by Leonardo.

Virgin of the Rocks, 1506–1508

DISCOVERIES

Botanists have spotted that the plants in the first version are typical of those that grow in dark, moist caves, whereas many of the plants in the second painting don't even exist. As Leonardo was so obsessed with representing nature realistically, it seems unlikely that he painted the plants in the second version. Most experts think that the second painting was started by Leonardo, but completed by his pupils, most likely the Predis brothers.

OR A DEVELOPMENT?

Other experts believe that Leonardo completed both paintings, and that in the second version he chose not to represent nature so accurately. They argue that it shows a development in his approach to painting, where he is choosing to be more imaginative and expressive in his work.

LIFE AND LEGACY

Leonardo spent the last three years of his life in France, as a guest of the French king, Francis I (1494–1547). During this time he went through his notes on painting in the hope of turning them into a book. It would take another 130 years before a small selection of these notes were published, continuing his influence on art long after his death.

The Deluge, c.1517–1518

END OF THE WORLD

Leonardo's final pieces of artwork appear as a series of drawings called *The Deluge*. They show a return to his fascination with the power of water. In *The Deluge* storms and waves violently crash down upon the Earth. It is as if they have come to wipe out all life, perhaps reflecting his thoughts on his own looming death. However, Leonardo still captures a sense of beauty and harmony in nature's patterns and shapes.

DEATH

Leonardo died on 2 May, 1519 in the arms of King Francis I, according to legend. He was buried in the chapel of the king's residence in Amboise, France. His faithful friend and pupil Melzi inherited most of his possessions, including around 8,000 pages of notes.

Portrait of a Bearded Man (believed to be a self-portrait) 1490s or 1512

'The loss of da Vinci saddened beyond all measure everyone who had known him, for no one ever lived who had brought so much honour to painting.'– Giorgio Vasari

DA VINCI TODAY

Leonardo's visions and explorations of the world surround us today, from his realised dreams of flying machines to updates of his anatomical drawings. His paintings introduced a new level of realism to art that still amazes viewers.

A CONTINUING LEGACY

In her 2014 *Walls of Water* series, Maggi Hambling (1945–) continues Leonardo's obsession in pinning down the essence of nature. Her giant crashing waves are full of movement and place the viewer in the action, experiencing both the beauty and terror of the natural world. These images are just as powerful as the waves drawn in Leonardo's *Deluge* series, and continue his explorations of nature's power in art.

The Death of Leonardo da Vinci, Ingres, 1818

Wall of Water VI, Maggi Hambling, 2014

TIMELINE

15 APRIL, 1452 Leonardo is born in Vinci, Italy

1467 sent to Florence to work as apprentice to Andrea del Verrocchio

1472–1475 paints *The Baptism of Christ* with Verrocchio, and *The Annunciation*

1473 draws *Landscape of the Arno Valley*

1474–1478 paints *Ginevra de' Benci*

1475 Michelangelo is born

1476 the *Portinari Altarpiece* by Hugo van der Goes arrives in Florence

1478 leaves Verrocchio's workshop

1478–1480 paints *Madonna of the Carnation*

c.1499 paints *Madonna of the Yarnwinder*

c.1480 paints *St Jerome in the Wilderness*

1481 begins work on *Adoration of the Magi*

1482 moves to Milan to work for Ludovico Sforza

1483 Raphael is born

1483–1486 paints the first *Virgin of the Rocks*

1489 begins work on the *Sforza Monument*

begins to study anatomy

1489–1490 paints *Lady with an Ermine*

Salaì comes to work for Leonardo

1492 draws *Vitruvian Man*

1495–1498 paints the *Last Supper*

1496 becomes a student and friend of mathematician Luca Pacioli

1499 the French army invades Milan

Leonardo leaves Milan and spends a short time in Venice

1499 begins work on *The Virgin and Child with St Anne and St John the Baptist*

1500 returns to Florence

1503 begins work on the *Mona Lisa*

1504 begins work on the mural *The Battle of Anghiari*

1506 Francesco Melzi comes to work for Leonardo

c.1506 paints *Leda and the Swan*

1506-1508 paints second *Virgin of the Rocks*

c.1508-1510 paints *Virgin with Child with St Anne*

1509 *On Divine Proportions* published, written by Luca Pacioli with illustrations by Leonardo

1513 moves to Rome

c.1513-1516 paints *St John the Baptist*

1516 the King of France invites Leonardo to come to work for him

c.1517–1518 work on a series of drawings known as *The Deluge*

2 MAY, 1519 dies in Cloux, France

SELECTED WORKS

Background information on some
of Leonardo's works:

THE ANNUNCIATION, C.1472–1475 (P.10)

The Annunciation, where the Angel Gabriel
appears before the Virgin Mary, was a popular
subject for 15th century Italian painters.
Leonardo's painting mainly follows the
standard layout used for this scene: the angel is
to the left, and Mary is to the right, interrupted
while reading from her prayer desk. However,
the background composition with the path
leading to a distant shipping scene and
landscape are of Leonardo's own design. This is
an early painting by him and the figures appear
awkwardly placed. The angel appears almost
flat, while the right arm of Mary has been
painted too long, but this is necessary for it to
reach over to her prayer book.

MADONNA OF THE CARNATION, 1478–1480 (P.15)

Leonardo's painting depicts the loving
relationship between Mary and the infant
Jesus. The hands of Jesus reach out, drawing
our attention to the carnation, but also to
Mary's brooch, which shows off Leonardo's skill
in painting light on a reflective surface. The
carnation is a symbol of Mary's love and purity,
but a red carnation can also be seen to
symbolise the future crucifixion of Jesus.
The vase is stuffed with irises, small lilies and
daisies, these flowers, along with the
transparency of the crystal vase, all symbolise
the purity of the Virgin Mary. The 16th century
writer Vasari praised the vase as 'being painted
with wonderful realism, which had on them
dewdrops that looked more convincing than the
real thing.'

ADORATION OF THE MAGI, 1481 (P.18)

Leonardo's unfinished painting shows how he
applied his first layers of colours – yellows,
rose brown and black – to help establish areas
of depth and the solidity of his shapes. This
painting is split into two areas of action and
time. The background portrays the Magi and
their men attempting to build tall structures
from which to view the star that would lead
them to Jesus. In the foreground they have
arrived at their destination and are kneeling
before Jesus and presenting their gifts. Mary is
at the centre of the image and appears as the
only still figure; she and Jesus are surrounded
by a semi-circle of action and dramatic
gestures, made more intense and passionate
by the dark washes of black shadow that shape
them.

ST JEROME IN THE WILDERNESS, C.1480 (P.22)

St Jerome went to live in the desert as a
rejection of modern life, choosing to spend his
time translating parts of the Bible and thinking
about death. Leonardo's painting shows
him with an expression of suffering, holding
out a rock he used to beat his chest with, as
punishment for un-Christian desires. He is
also pictured with a lion, which became his
companion when he pulled a thorn out from its
paw. The painting was meant for an altarpiece,
but was left unfinished. Many years later it
would end up in two pieces – a square section
around the head had at some point been cut out
and was found being used as a table.

GLOSSARY

accurate when something is correct, such as a truthful representation in art

aerial perspective a technique that creates a sense of distance in painting by using different shades of blue and blurring the outline of objects furthest away from the viewer

anatomical relating to the anatomy, which is the scientific study of the structure and biology of the body

apprentice a person who is learning a new skill or job by working for an expert in that profession

astronomy the scientific study of the stars, planets and other objects in outer space

atmosphere the air or gases that surround us

botanist a scientist who specialises in the study of plants

chiaroscuro a technique suggesting volume or mood by exaggerating the contrast between light and dark areas in a painting or drawing

commission where a person or an organisation asks an artist to produce work in return for paying a fee

composition how all the elements of an image, such as a painting, fit together

deluge a great flood of water

depiction a representation of something made in a drawing or painting

dispute a disagreement or an argument usually relating to matters of business

dissect to cut something apart, such as a plant or animal, to examine the inside of its body for science

divine a quality of beauty similar to ideas of harmony in religious beliefs

elements things that make up the natural environment, including earth, air and water

engineering the use of science and technology in the design and building of machines and structures such as bridges

explorations the action of travel or study to discover something new, such as unfamiliar lands or experiments in the arts or science

forefront to be in a leading position; one of the first to experience something new

foreground the part of an image that appears closest to the viewer

formula a set rule of mathematical symbols and numbers used to find something out

Futurism an artistic movement that started in Italy in about 1909. Its artists were inspired by, and tried to express, the dynamism of contemporary life and the speed and force of modern machinery

genius someone who is highly intelligent and talented, including artists that show a level of original creativity that is greater than other artists

geometry the mathematical study of shapes, points, lines, curves and surfaces

golden ratio a calculation used to create shapes and divisions of space in art and architecture that are believed to be pleasing to the eye and produce a sense of natural harmony. Often found in nature

grotesque something that looks very ugly, almost unnatural and sometimes comical

Holy Trinity the union of three forms of God from Christian religion: the Father, the Son and the Holy Spirit

horizon the line where sky and earth or sea seem to meet

hydraulics involving equipment or machinery that is powered by putting a fluid, such as water or oil, under pressure

icon an image of a person or a thing that becomes a representative symbol and is used as a celebration of what it represents

ideal something that is perfect or exists in the imagination as perfect but may not exist in real life

illegitimate born of parents who are not married to each other

internal organs parts of a living thing that are inside its body, such as your heart and lungs

monument a statue, building or other structure that is used to represent the memory of someone or of a great event

mural a large painting on a wall

natural processes the action of changes in nature that make the world what it is, such as the water cycle

obsession being continually focused on one thing, with a passion for one object or area of study

opaque describes a surface or material that you are not able to see through

patronage the act of giving support, usually with money, for the return of work or the satisfaction and fame in having helped a successful person or project

perspective the art of drawing solid objects and creating a sense of space and depth on a flat surface, providing an illusion of distance to the viewer

perspective grid a network of lines used to help plan out a sense of distance within a drawing or painting

philosophical idea an idea about truth, nature and the meaning of life

pigment natural colouring from plants, rocks or animals that is used in the creation of colours in paints

Pop art an art movement that was inspired by themes and styles of popular modern culture, such as comic strips and advertising

pose the deliberate positioning of a person's body for a painting or drawing

Pre-Raphaelite a member of the Pre-Raphaelite Brotherhood, a group of artists from 19th century England that aimed to revive the style and spirit of Italian art from before the time of the painter Raphael

proportions the arrangement of parts that form a whole; proportions are sometimes used as measurements to work out the size of the part in relation to the whole

pyramidal pose a pose used in paintings and drawings with people or objects positioned in a three-dimensional triangle shape, like a pyramid

realism an attempt in art or literature to be true to life as we know it, not as we might wish or imagine it to be

Renaissance the word means 'renewal', and is used to describe a period that began in Italy in the early 15th century before spreading throughout Europe by about 1600. It was a time when the study of ancient Roman and Greek culture combined with new discoveries in the sciences, technology, and commerce to create new social and artistic movements

restoration to bring something back to its former state, such as repairing a broken sculpture

sfumato as if seen through smoke or vapour; where hard edges between colours or light and dark areas are smudged

subtle something that appears faint, delicate and hard to see

surreal showing something dreamlike and unfamiliar; having come from the unconscious mind or from a dream

symbol an object used to represent something that cannot be seen, such as an idea or feeling

tempera a method of painting using water-based, opaque pigments made with egg yolks, that was widely used up until the end of the 15th century when oil paints became more popular

three-dimensional having the appearance of being a real, solid, physical form, with length, depth and breadth

translucent allowing light to pass through it

vanishing point the point on a painting or drawing at which the lines of perspective meet, acting as the further point in the distance where objects stop being visible

X-rays pictures taken using electromagnetic radiation to see inside something, such as the human body or layers hidden beneath the surface of a painting

INDEX

FURTHER INFORMATION

BOOKS:

Eyewitness: Leonardo da Vinci by Andrew Langley (Dorling Kindersley, 2006)

In the Picture with: Leonardo da Vinci by Ian Zaczek (Wayland, 2014)

Leonardo da Vinci: Complete Paintings and Drawings by Frank Zollner and Johannes Nathan (Tashcen, 2011)

WEBSITES:

Website that explores in detail the many different inventions of Leonardo with links to modern-day counterparts: **www.da-vinci-inventions.com**

A short biography of Leonardo from the National Gallery alongside links to some of his paintings, with accompanying information, from their collection: **www.nationalgallery.org.uk/artists/leonardo-da-vinci**

A highly comprehensive website that explores the life and work of Leonardo through a timeline, as well as through themed 'trails', with games, images and text that help understand the techniques and science behind much of his work: **www.universalleonardo.org/index.php**